AWS Certified Cloud Practitioner Practice Tests 2023: 200+ AWS Practice Exam Questions with Answers

By Manish Thakurani

Table of Contents

Preview of Questions

1. Which of the following is a fast and reliable NoSQL database service?

    A. Amazon Redshift

    B. Amazon DynamoDB

    C. Amazon RDS

    D. Amazon S3

Answer: B. Amazon DynamoDB

2. Which design principles for cloud architecture are recommended when re-architecting a large monolithic application? (Select TWO.)

    A. Use manual monitoring.

    B. Use fixed servers.

    C. Implement loose coupling.

    D. Rely on individual components.

    E. Design for scalability

Answer: D. Rely on individual E. Design for scalability

3. A customer needs to run a MySQL database that easily scales. Which AWS service should they use?

    A. Amazon Redshift

    B. Amazon DynamoDB

    C. Amazon Aurora

    D. Amazon ElastiCache

Answer: C. Amazon Aurora

Cloud Computing

Cloud computing is the on-demand delivery of IT resources over the Internet with pay-as-you-go pricing. Instead of buying, owning, and maintaining physical data centers and servers, you can access technology services, such as computing power, storage, and databases, on an as-needed basis from a cloud provider like Amazon Web Services (AWS).

Benefits of cloud computing

Agility

The cloud gives you easy access to a broad range of technologies so that you can innovate faster and build nearly anything that you can imagine. You can quickly spin up resources as you need them–from infrastructure services, such as compute, storage, and databases, to Internet of Things, machine learning, data lakes and analytics, and much more.

You can deploy technology services in a matter of minutes, and get from idea to implementation several orders of magnitude faster than before. This gives you the freedom to experiment, test new ideas to differentiate customer experiences, and transform your business.

Elasticity

With cloud computing, you don't have to over-provision resources up front to handle peak levels of business activity in the future. Instead, you provision the amount of resources that you actually need. You can scale these resources up or down to instantly grow and shrink capacity as your business needs change.

Cost savings

The cloud allows you to trade fixed expenses (such as data centers and physical servers) for variable expenses, and only pay for IT as you consume it. Plus, the variable expenses are much lower than what you would pay to do it yourself because of the economies of scale.

Deploy globally in minutes

With the cloud, you can expand to new geographic regions and deploy globally in minutes. For example, AWS has infrastructure all over the world, so you can deploy your application in multiple physical locations with just a few clicks. Putting applications in closer proximity to end users reduces latency and improves their experience.

Types of cloud computing

Infrastructure as a Service (IaaS)

IaaS contains the basic building blocks for cloud IT. It typically provides access to networking features, computers (virtual or on dedicated hardware), and data storage space. IaaS gives you the highest level of flexibility and management control over your IT resources. It is most similar to the existing IT resources with which many IT departments and developers are familiar.

Platform as a Service (PaaS)

PaaS removes the need for you to manage underlying infrastructure (usually hardware and operating systems), and allows you to focus on the deployment and management of your applications. This helps you be more efficient as you don't need to worry about resource procurement, capacity planning, software maintenance, patching, or any of the other undifferentiated heavy lifting involved in running your application.

Software as a Service (SaaS)

SaaS provides you with a complete product that is run and managed by the service provider. In most cases, people referring to SaaS are referring to end-user applications (such as web-based email). With a SaaS offering, you don't have to think about how the service is maintained or how the underlying infrastructure is managed. You only need to think about how you will use that particular software.

Dynamo DB

✓ Handle more than 10 trillion requests per day and can support peaks of more than 20 million requests per second.
✓ Secure your data with encryption at rest, automatic backup and restore, and guaranteed reliability with an SLA of up to 99.999% availability.
✓ Focus on innovation and optimize costs with a fully managed serverless database that automatically scales up and down to fit your needs.
✓ Integrate with AWS services to do more with your data. Use built-in tools to perform analytics, extract insights, and monitor traffic trends.

Use Cases of Dynamo DB

- **Retail**
  Companies in the retail space use DynamoDB to deliver low latency for mission-critical use cases. Scaling up and down allows these customers to pay only for the capacity they need and keeps precious technical resources focused on innovations rather than operations.

- **Banking & Finance**
  Companies in banking and finance use DynamoDB to increase agility, reduce time to market, and minimize operational overhead while maintaining the security and reliability of their applications.

- **Software & Internet**
  DynamoDB has a proven record of being able to handle internet-scale use cases and their requirements while maintaining consistent, single-digit millisecond latency. With global tables, DynamoDB customers can easily expand their applications to multiple AWS Regions for global reach and business continuity.

Architecting for Reliable Scalability

Generally, a solution or service's reliability is influenced by its up time, performance, security, manageability, etc. To achieve reliability in the context of scale, take into consideration the following primary design principals.

Modularity

Modularity aims to break a complex component or solution into smaller parts that are less complicated and easier to scale, secure, and manage.

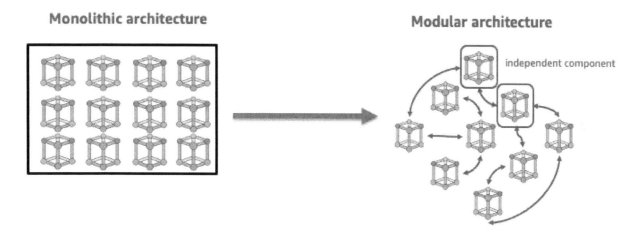

Figure 1: Monolithic Architecture (Source: https://aws.amazon.com/blogs/architecture/architecting-for-reliable-scalability/)

Modular design is commonly used in modern application developments. where an application's software is constructed of multiple and loosely coupled building blocks (functions). These functions collectively integrate through pre-defined common interfaces or APIs to form the desired application functionality (commonly referred to as microservices architecture).

Horizontal scaling

A "horizontally scalable" system is one that can increase capacity by adding more computers to the system. This is in contrast to a "vertically scalable" system, which is constrained to running its processes on only one computer; in such systems the only way to increase performance is to add more resources into one computer in the form of faster (or more) CPUs, memory or storage.

Horizontally scalable systems are oftentimes able to outperform vertically scalable systems by enabling parallel execution of workloads and distributing those across many different computers.

This principle can be complemented with a modularity design principle, in which the scaling model can be applied to certain component(s) or microservice(s) of the application stack. For example, only scale-out Amazon Elastic Cloud Compute (EC2) front-end web instances that reside behind an Elastic Load Balancing (ELB) layer with auto-scaling groups. In contrast, this elastic horizontal scalability might be very difficult to achieve for a monolithic type of application.

Horizontal Scaling

Add more resources like virtual machines to your system to spread out the workload across them.

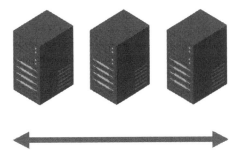

- Increases high availability

- Fewer periods of downtime

- Easy to resize according to your needs

Figure 2: Horizontal Scaling (Source: stromit.cloud)

Benefits of horizontal scaling

Horizontal scaling **increases high availability** because as long as you are spreading your infrastructure across multiple areas, if one machine fails, you can just use one of the other ones.

Because you're adding a machine, you need **fewer periods of downtime** and don't have to switch the old machine off while scaling. There may never be a need for downtime if you scale effectively.

- And here are some simpler advantages of horizontal scaling:
- Easy to resize according to your needs
- Immediate and continuous availability
- Cost can be linked to usage, and you don't always have to pay for peak demand

Disadvantages of horizontal scaling

The main disadvantage of horizontal scaling is that it **increases the complexity of the maintenance and operations** of your architecture, but there are services in the AWS environment to solve this issue.

- Architecture design and deployment can be very complicated
- A limited amount of software that can take advantage of horizontal scaling

Vertical Scaling

Through vertical scaling (scaling up or down), you can increase or decrease the capacity of existing services/instances by upgrading the memory (RAM), storage, or processing power (CPU). Usually, this means that the expansion has an upper limit based on the capacity of the server or machine being expanded.

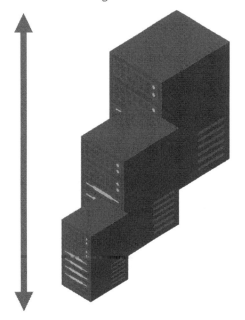

Vertical Scaling

Increase or decrease the capacity of existing services/instances.

- No changes have to be made to the application code

- Less complex network

- Less complicated maintenance

Figure 3: Vertical Scaling (Source: stromit.cloud)

Vertical scaling benefits

- **No changes must be made to the application code** and no additional servers need to be added; you just make the server you have more powerful or downsize again.
- **Less complex network** – when a single instance handles all the layers of your services, it will not have to synchronize and communicate with other machines to work. This may result in faster responses.
- **Less complicated maintenance** – the maintenance is easier and less complex because of the number of instances you will need to manage.

Vertical scaling disadvantages

- **A maintenance window with downtime is required** – unless you have a backup server that can handle operations and requests, you will need some considerable downtime to upgrade your machine.
- **Single point of failure** – having all your operations on a single server increases the risk of losing all your data if a hardware or software failure were to occur.
- **Upgrade limitations** – there is a limitation to how much you can upgrade a machine/instance.

Horizontal scaling vs. vertical scaling

In the cloud, you will usually use both methods, but horizontal scaling is usually considered a long-term solution, while vertical scaling is usually considered a short-term solution. The reason for this distinction is that you can usually add as many servers to the infrastructure as you need, but sometimes hardware upgrades are just not possible anymore.

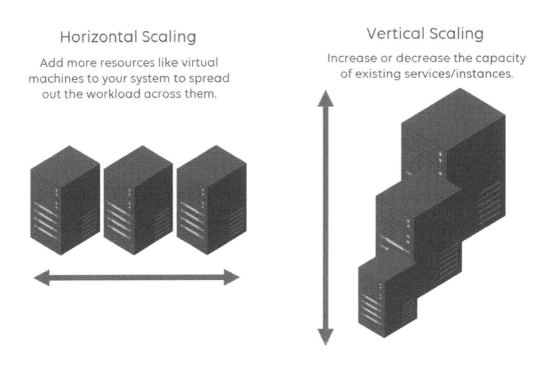

Figure 4: Horizontal Scaling vs Vertical Scaling

Both horizontal and vertical scaling have their benefits and limitations. Here are some factors to consider:

- **Worldwide distribution** – if you plan to have national or global customers, it is unreasonable to expect them to access your services from one location. In this case, you need to scale resources horizontally.
- **Reliability and availability** – horizontal scaling can provide you with a more reliable system. It increases redundancy and ensures that you are not dependent on one machine.
- **Performance** – sometimes it's better to leave the application as is and upgrade the hardware to meet demand (vertically scale). Horizontal scaling may require you to rewrite code, which can add complexity.

AWS CloudFormation

AWS CloudFormation is a service that enables developers to create AWS resources in an orderly and predictable fashion. Resources are written in text files using JSON or YAML format. The templates require a specific syntax and structure that depends on the types of resources being created and managed. You author your resources in JSON or YAML with any code editor such as AWS Cloud9, check it into a version control system, and then CloudFormation builds the specified services in safe, repeatable manner.

A CloudFormation template is deployed into the AWS environment as a stack. You can manage stacks through the AWS Management Console, AWS Command Line Interface, or AWS CloudFormation APIs. If you need to make changes to the running resources in a stack you update the stack. Before making changes to your resources, you can generate a change set, which is a summary of your proposed changes. Change sets enable you to see how your changes might impact your running resources, especially for critical resources, before implementing them.

AWS Shared Responsibility Model

Security is a shared responsibility between AWS and the customer. The different parts of the Shared

Responsibility Model are:

- **AWS responsibility "Security of the Cloud"** - AWS is responsible for protecting the infrastructure that runs all of the services offered in the AWS Cloud. This infrastructure is composed of the hardware, software, networking, and facilities that run AWS Cloud services

- **Customer responsibility "Security in the Cloud"** – Customer responsibility is determined by the AWS Cloud services that a customer selects. This determines the amount of configuration work the customer must perform as part of their security responsibilities

Identity and Access Management

AWS Identity and Access Management (IAM) defines the controls and polices that are used to manage access to AWS resources. Using IAM you can create users and groups and define permissions to various DevOps services.

In addition to the users, various services may also need access to AWS resources. For example, your CodeBuild project might need access to store Docker images in Amazon Elastic Container Registry (Amazon ECR) and need permissions to write to Amazon ECR. These types of permissions are defined by a special type role know as service role.

IAM is one component of the AWS security infrastructure. With IAM, you can centrally manage groups, users, service roles and security credentials such as passwords, access keys, and permissions policies that control which AWS services and resources users can access. IAM Policy lets you define the set of permissions. This policy can then be attached to either a role, user, or a service to define their permission.

You can also use IAM to create roles that are used widely within your desired DevOps strategy. In some cases, it can make perfect sense to programmatically AssumeRole instead of directly getting the permissions. When a service or user assumes roles, they are given temporary credentials to access a service that they normally don't have access to.

How can users access AWS

1. AWS Mgmt Console (protected by password + MFA)
2. AWS CLI (protected by access keys) – AWS CloudShell is CLI within browser
3. AWS SDK – for code – protected by access keys

Virtual MFA device – Google authenticator (phone only), Authy (multi-device)

Physical devices: U2F key. Gemalto- h/w key fob MFA device, SurePass Id for US govt

Regions

AWS has the concept of a Region, which is a physical location around the world where we cluster data centers. We call each group of logical data centers an Availability Zone (aka AZ). Each AWS Region consists of a minimum of three, isolated, and physically separate AZs within a geographic area. Unlike other cloud providers, who often define a region as a single data center, the multiple AZ design of every AWS Region offers advantages for customers. Each AZ has independent power, cooling, and physical security and is connected via redundant, ultra-low-latency networks. AWS customers focused on high availability can design their applications to run in multiple AZs to achieve even greater fault-tolerance. AWS infrastructure Regions meet the highest levels of security, compliance, and data protection.

Availability Zone

An Availability Zone (AZ) is one or more discrete data centers with redundant power, networking, and connectivity in an AWS Region. AZs give customers the ability to operate production applications and databases that are more highly available, fault tolerant, and scalable than would be possible from a single data center. All AZs in an AWS Region are interconnected with high-bandwidth, low-latency networking, over fully redundant, dedicated metro fiber providing high-throughput, low-latency networking between AZs. All traffic between AZs is encrypted. The network performance is sufficient to accomplish synchronous replication between AZs. AZs make partitioning applications for high availability easy. If an application is partitioned across AZs, companies are better isolated and protected from issues such as power outages, lightning strikes, tornadoes, earthquakes, and more. AZs are physically separated by a meaningful distance, many kilometers, from any other AZ, although all are within 100 km (60 miles) of each other.

Amazon S3

Amazon Simple Storage Service (Amazon S3) is an object storage service that offers industry-leading scalability, data availability, security, and performance. Customers of all sizes and industries can use Amazon S3 to store and protect any amount of data for a range of use cases, such as data lakes, websites, mobile applications, backup and restore, archive, enterprise applications, IoT devices, and big data analytics. Amazon S3 provides management features so that you can optimize, organize, and configure access to your data to meet your specific business, organizational, and compliance requirements.

Features:

- S3 is a safe place to store the files.
- It is Object-based storage, i.e., you can store the images, word files, pdf files, etc.
- The files which are stored in S3 can be from 0 Bytes to 5 TB.
- It has unlimited storage means that you can store the data as much you want.
- Files are stored in Bucket. A bucket is like a folder available in S3 that stores the files.
- S3 is a universal namespace, i.e., the names must be unique globally. Bucket contains a DNS address. Therefore, the bucket must contain a unique name to generate a unique DNS address.

Amazon EC2

Amazon Elastic Compute Cloud (Amazon EC2) provides on-demand, scalable computing capacity in the Amazon Web Services (AWS) Cloud. Using Amazon EC2 reduces hardware costs so you can develop and deploy applications faster. You can use Amazon EC2 to launch as many or as few virtual servers as you need, configure security and networking, and manage storage. You can add capacity (scale up) to handle compute-heavy tasks, such as monthly or yearly processes, or spikes in website traffic. When usage decreases, you can reduce capacity (scale down) again.

The EC2 instance is secured with a security group, which is a virtual firewall that controls incoming and outgoing traffic. A private key is stored on the local computer and a public key is stored on the instance. Both keys are specified as a key pair to prove the identity of the user. In this scenario, the instance is backed by an Amazon EBS volume. The VPC communicates with the internet using an internet gateway.

AWS EC2 Instance Types:

- On-demand instances
- Reserved instances
- Scheduled reserved instances
- Spot instances
- Dedicated hosts

On-Demand Instances

On-demand computing instances are computing instances that are available when needed. On-demand instances are charged by either the second or hour of use, and facilitate autoscaling. This means these instances can grow on demand by adding additional instances. On-demand instances are optimal when reliable computing capacity is needed without complete knowledge of how long the application will be used or its capacity requirements.

Reserved Instances

A reserved instance is an instance where an organization commits to purchase a specified compute capacity for a specified period of time. It is essentially a contract to purchase a computing instance and can be for one to three years. By purchasing instances based upon long-term use, the organization can receive substantial savings over on-demand pricing. Reserved instances are optimal when an organization knows how long the application will be used and its capacity requirements.

Scheduled Reserved Instances

A scheduled reserved instance is a special type of reserved instance. This type of instance is optimal when you have a need for a specific amount of computing power on a scheduled basis. For example, if an organization has a mission-critical batch job that runs every Saturday and Sunday.

Spot Instances

A spot instance is an instance that is pulled from unused AWS capacity. Spot instances are sold in an auction-like manner in which an organization places a bid. If the bid price is equal to or greater than the spot price, a spot instance is purchased. Spot instances are deeply discounted and can be a great option. The drawback of spot instances is that they can be terminated if the spot price goes above the price that was bid on the instances. Spot instances are ideal when an organization needs extra computing capacity at a great price for non-mission-critical use.

Amazon EBS

Amazon EBS (or Elastic Block Store) is a product designed to mimic this exact scenario. It works with Amazon Elastic Compute Cloud (or EC2), so all of the storage is available in the cloud, yet it uses block storage in the same way you would expect if you had local drives and servers in a data center. That means your staff can create storage volumes as though they are in a data center as opposed to the more typical object storage method. (Object storage is more "elastic" in that files also contain metadata and identifiers, which means they can reside anywhere on a volume such that apps rely on the file pointers for accessing the data.)

With block storage, each volume acts as an actual raw data storage volume that can be mounted and used as though it is a local drive. Each of these volumes can be up to 16TB in size, and you can create and manage your own file system on the drives.

AWS Trusted Advisor

AWS Trusted Advisor is a service that inspects all the resources present in your AWS account and suggests improvements to bring them in line with AWS best practices.

When you first start using AWS it is reasonably easy to keep track of what you have running, however as time goes on and your account footprint grows you may start to get sub-optimal scenarios in terms of cost management and performance that go unnoticed.

You may have orphaned resources, unused or obsolete snapshots, storage volumes that are no longer in use, resources that are not attached to instances, the list goes on and these resources are costing your business money. You may also have resources configured that aren't optimized for security, performance or fault tolerance.

Trusted Advisor checks five categories of best practice compliance being cost optimization, performance, security, fault tolerance and service limits.

Figure 5: Trust Advisor Categories (Source: https://www.hava.io/)

List of Common AWS Services

Name	Full Form	Description
Amazon Aurora	Amazon Aurora	Amazon Aurora is a relational database management system (RDBMS) built for the cloud with full MySQL and PostgreSQL compatibility.
Amazon Cognito	Amazon Cognito	AWS Cognito administers a control access dashboard for on-boarding users through sign-up, and sign-in features to their web and mobile apps.
Amazon EC2	Elastic Compute Cloud	EC2 is a cloud platform provided by Amazon that offers secure, and resizable compute capacity. Its purpose is to enable easy access and usability to developers for web-scale cloud computing, while allowing for total control of your compute resources.
Amazon EBS	Elastic Block Store	Amazon Elastic Block Store (Amazon EBS) provides block level storage volumes for use with EC2 instances
Amazon ElastiCache	Amazon ElastiCache	ElastiCache is an AWS service that effortlessly sets up, runs, and scales popular open-source, in-memory data storages in the cloud. Operate data-intensive apps or enhance the performance of existing databases by evaluating data from high throughput and low latency in-memory data stores.
Amazon Glacier	Amazon Glacier	AWS Glacier services are secure, flexible, and affordable Amazon S3 cloud storage classes for data caching and prolonged backup.
Amazon IAM	Identity and Access Management	AWS Identity and Access Management provides secure access and management of resources in a secure and compliant manner. By leveraging IAM, you can create and manage users and groups by allowing and denying

		their permissions for individual resources.
Amazon Lambda	Amazon Lambda	Lambda permits you to run code without owning or managing servers. Users only pay for the compute time consumed.
Amazon RDS	Relational Database Services	Amazon Relational Database Service (Amazon RDS) makes database configuration, management, and scaling easy in the cloud. Automate tedious tasks such as hardware provisioning, database arrangement, patching, and backups – cost-effectively and proportionate to your needs.
Amazon Route 53	Amazon Route 53	Amazon Route 53 is a highly available and scalable Domain Name System (DNS) web service.
Amazon S3	Simple Storage Service	Amazon S3, at its core, facilitates object storage, providing leading scalability, data availability, security, and performance. Businesses of vast sizes can leverage S3 for storage and protect large sums of data for various use cases, such as websites, applications, backup, and more.
Amazon SNS	Simple Notification Service	Amazon SNS is a fully managed messaging solution that provides low-cost infrastructure for bulk message delivery, primarily to mobile users
Amazon SQS	Simple Queue Service	AWS SQS is a fully managed message queuing facility enabling you to decouple and scale microservices, distributed systems, and serverless apps. SQS purges the intricacies and overhead associated with managing and operating message-oriented middleware and permits developers to focus on diverse workloads.

Amazon VPC	Virtual Private Cloud	Amazon VPC enables you to set up a reasonably isolated section of the AWS Cloud where you can deploy AWS resources at scale in a virtual environment.
AWS Amplify	AWS Amplify	AWS Amplify is a suite of purpose-built tools and capabilities meant to make building full-stack applications on AWS simpler for front-end web and mobile developers.
AWS CFT	Cloud Formation Template	Cloudformation is designed to tackle software-defined infrastructure - an IT setup where developers or operations teams continuously manage and provision the technological stack for an application via software, rather than manually configuring separate hardware devices and operating systems.
AWS Management Console	AWS Management Console	The AWS Management Console provides everything needed for running an application on a single interface.
AWS Rekognition	AWS Rekognition	Computer vision (CV) capabilities provided by Amazon Rekognition are pre-trained and programmable, making it easy to extract data and insights from images and videos.
Dynamo DB	Dynamo DB	DynamoDB is a document database with key-value structuring that delivers single-digit millisecond performance at scale. Dynamo has built-in security with a fully managed, multimaster, multiregion, durable database, backup and restore, and in-memory archiving for web-scale applications.
Load balancer	Load balancer	A load balancer serves as the single point of contact for clients. The load balancer distributes incoming application traffic across multiple targets, such as EC2 instances, in multiple Availability Zones.

Exam Overview

Domain Weightage:

Sr.	Domain	% of Exam
1	Cloud Concepts	26%
2	Security Concepts	25%
3	Technology	33%
4	Billing and Pricing	16%
	Total	100%

Category	Foundational
Exam duration	90 minutes
Exam format	65 questions; either multiple choice or multiple response
Cost	100 USD
Test in-person or online	Pearson VUE testing center or online proctored exam
Languages offered	English, Japanese, Korean, Simplified Chinese, Traditional Chinese, Bahasa (Indonesian), Spanish (Spain), Spanish (Latin America), French (France), German, Italian, and Portuguese (Brazil)

Practice Questions with Answers

1. Which of the following is a fast and reliable NoSQL database service?
    A. Amazon Redshift
    B. Amazon DynamoDB
    C. Amazon RDS
    D. Amazon S3
Answer: B. Amazon DynamoDB

2. Which design principles for cloud architecture are recommended when re-architecting a large monolithic application? (Select TWO.)
    A. Use manual monitoring.
    B. Use fixed servers.
    C. Implement loose coupling.
    D. Rely on individual components.
    E. Design for scalability
Answer: D. Rely on individual E. Design for scalability

3. A customer needs to run a MySQL database that easily scales. Which AWS service should they use?
    A. Amazon Redshift
    B. Amazon DynamoDB
    C. Amazon Aurora
    D. Amazon ElastiCache
Answer: C. Amazon Aurora

4. A company is considering using AWS for a self-hosted database that requires a nightly shutdown for maintenance and cost-saving purposes. Which service should the company use?

    A. Amazon EC2 with Amazon Elastic Block Store (Amazon EBS)
    B. Amazon DynamoDB
    C. Amazon Redshift
    D. Amazon Elastic Compute Cloud (Amazon EC2) with Amazon EC2 instance store

Answer: A. Amazon EC2 with Amazon Elastic Block Store (Amazon EBS)

5. A company is migrating an application that is running non-interruptible workloads for a three-year time frame. Which pricing construct would provide the MOST cost-effective solution?

    A. Amazon EC2 Spot Instances
    B. Amazon EC2 On-Demand Instances
    C. Amazon EC2 Reserved Instances
    D. Amazon EC2 Dedicated Instances

Answer: D. Amazon EC2 Dedicated Instances

6. Which of the following components of the AWS Global Infrastructure consists of one or more discrete data centers interconnected through low latency links?

    A. Region
    B. Private networking
    C. Availability Zone
    D. Edge location

Answer: A. Region

7. Which AWS Cost Management tool allows you to view the most granular data about your AWS bill?

    A. AWS Cost Explorer
    B. AWS Budgets
    C. AWS Cost and Usage report
    D. AWS Billing dashboard

Answer: C. AWS Cost and Usage report

8. Which AWS services should be used for read/write of constantly changing data? (Select TWO.)
    A. Amazon RDS
    B. Amazon Redshift
    C. Amazon Glacier
    D. AWS Snowball
    E. Amazon EFS

Answer: A, B

9. How do customers benefit from Amazon's massive economies of scale?

    A. Periodic price reductions as the result of Amazon's operational efficiencies
    B. New Amazon EC2 instance types providing the latest hardware
    C. The ability to scale up and down when needed
    D. Increased reliability in the underlying hardware of Amazon EC2 instances

Answer: C. The ability to scale up and down when needed

10. Under the shared responsibility model, which of the following is the customer responsible for?

A. Ensuring that disk drives are wiped after use.

B. Ensuring that firmware is updated on hardware devices.

C. Ensuring that data is encrypted at rest.

D. Ensuring that network cables are category six or higher.

Answer: C. Ensuring that data is encrypted at rest.

11. Which of the following security-related actions are available at no cost?

A. Calling AWS Support

B. Attending AWS classes at a local university

C. Contacting AWS Professional Services to request a workshop

D. Accessing forums, blogs, and whitepapers

Answer: D. Accessing forums, blogs, and whitepapers

12. Which is a recommended pattern for designing a highly available architecture on AWS?

A. Run enough Amazon EC2 instances to operate at peak load.

B. Ensure that the application is designed to accommodate failure of any single component.

C. Use a monolithic application that handles all operations.

D. Ensure that components have low-latency network connectivity

Answer: B. Ensure that the application is designed to accommodate failure of any single component.

13. A characteristic of edge locations is that they:

A. help lower latency and improve performance for users.

B. cache frequently changing data without reaching the origin server.

C. host Amazon EC2 instances closer to users.

D. refresh data changes daily.

Answer: B. cache frequently changing data without reaching the origin server.

14. What is the benefit of using AWS managed services, such as Amazon ElastiCache and Amazon Relational Database Service (Amazon RDS)?

A. They simplify patching and updating underlying OSs.

B. They do not require the customer to optimize instance type or size selections.

C. They have better performance than customer-managed services.

D. They require the customer to monitor and replace failing instances.

Answer: B. They do not require the customer to optimize instance type or size selections.

15. The use of what AWS feature or service allows companies to track and categorize spending on a detailed level?

A. AWS Marketplace

B. AWS Budgets

C. Consolidated billing

D. Cost allocation tags

Answer: D. Cost allocation tags

16. Which of the following is an AWS Cloud architecture design principle?

A. Implement single points of failure.

B. Implement loose coupling.

C. Implement monolithic design.

D. Implement vertical scaling.

Answer: B. Implement loose coupling.

17. Where can AWS compliance and certification reports be downloaded?

A. AWS Artifact

B. AWS Concierge

C. AWS Certificate Manager

D. AWS Trusted Advisor

Answer: A. AWS Artifact

18. A company is looking for a scalable data warehouse solution. Which of the following AWS solutions would meet the company's needs?
   A. Amazon DynamoDB
   B. Amazon Simple Storage Service (Amazon S3)
   C. Amazon Kinesis
   D. Amazon Redshift
Answer: D. Amazon Redshift

19. Which of the following AWS features enables a user to launch a pre-configured Amazon Elastic Compute Cloud (Amazon EC2) instance?
   A. Amazon Elastic Block Store (Amazon EBS)
   B. Amazon Machine Image
   C. Amazon EC2 Systems Manager
   D. Amazon AppStream 2.0
Answer: B. Amazon Machine Image

20. AWS supports which of the following methods to add security to Identity and Access Management (IAM) users? (Select TWO.)
   A. Using AWS Shield-protected resources
   B. Using Multi-Factor Authentication (MFA)
   C. Blocking access with Security Groups
   D. Implementing Amazon Rekognition
   E. Enforcing password strength and expiration
Answer: B, E

21. Which of the following security-related services does AWS offer? (Select TWO.)

   A. Multi-factor authentication physical tokens
   B. AWS Trusted Advisor security checks
   C. Automated penetration testing
   D. Data encryption
   E. Amazon S3 copyrighted content detection
Answer: A, D

22. Under the shared responsibility model, which of the following is a shared control between a customer and AWS?

    A. Physical controls

    B. Patch management

    C. Zone security

    D. Data center auditing

Answer: B. Patch management

23. How does AWS shorten the time to provision IT resources?

    A. It supplies an online IT ticketing platform for resource requests.

    B. It automates the resource request process from a company's IT vendor list.

    C. It supports automatic code validation services.

    D. It provides the ability to programmatically provision existing resources.

Answer: D. It provides the ability to programmatically provision existing resources.

24. Which of the following common IT tasks can AWS cover to free up company IT resources? (Select TWO.)

    A. Creating database schema

    B. Testing application releases

    C. Patching databases software

    D. Running penetration tests

    E. Backing up databases

Answer: C, E

25. Under the shared responsibility model, which of the following tasks are the responsibility of the AWS customer? (Select TWO.)

   A. Ensuring that users have received security training in the use of AWS services

   B. Ensuring that access to data centers is restricted

   C. Ensuring that hardware is disposed of properly

   D. Ensuring that AWS NTP servers are set to the correct time

   E. Ensuring that application data is encrypted at rest

Answer: A, E

26. Which of the following services will automatically scale with an expected increase in web traffic?   A. AWS CodePipeline

   B. Amazon EBS

   C. AWS Direct Connect

   D. Elastic Load Balancing

Answer: D. Elastic Load Balancing

27. Which of the following is a component of the shared responsibility model managed entirely by AWS?

   A. Patching operating system software

   B. Encrypting data

   C. Enforcing multi-factor authentication

   D. Auditing physical data center assets

Answer: D. Auditing physical data center assets

28. Which Amazon EC2 pricing model adjusts based on supply and demand of EC2 instances?

   A. On-Demand Instances

   B. Reserved Instances

   C. Spot Instances

   D. Convertible Reserved Instances

Answer: C. Spot Instances

29. Which of the following inspects AWS environments to find opportunities that can save money for users and also improve system performance?

A. AWS Cost Explorer

B. Consolidated billing

C. Detailed billing

D. AWS Trusted Advisor

Answer: D. AWS Trusted Advisor

30. One of the advantages to moving infrastructure from an on-premises data center to the AWS Cloud is:

A. it allows the business to focus on business activities.

B. it allows the business to put a server in each customer's data center.

C. it allows the business to eliminate IT bills.

D. it allows the business to leave servers unpatched.

Answer: A. it allows the business to focus on business activities.

31. Which task is AWS responsible for in the shared responsibility model for security and compliance?

A. Granting access to individuals and services

B. Encrypting data in transit

C. Updating Amazon EC2 host firmware

D. Updating operating systems

Answer: C. Updating Amazon EC2 host firmware

32. A company wants to reduce the physical compute footprint that developers use to run code. Which service would meet that need by enabling serverless architectures?

A. Amazon Elastic Compute Cloud (Amazon EC2)

B. AWS Lambda

C. Amazon DynamoDB

D. AWS CodeCommit

Answer: B. AWS Lambda

33. A customer would like to design and build a new workload on AWS Cloud but does not have the AWS-related software technical expertise in-house. Which of the following AWS programs can a customer take advantage of to achieve that outcome?

A. AWS Partner Network Technology Partners

B. AWS Marketplace

C. AWS Partner Network Consulting Partners

D. AWS Service Catalog

Answer: C. AWS Partner Network Consulting Partners

34. How can an AWS user with an AWS Basic Support plan obtain technical assistance from AWS?

A. AWS Senior Support Engineers

B. AWS Technical Account Managers

C. AWS Trusted Advisor

D. AWS Discussion Forums

Answer: C. AWS Trusted Advisor

35. Which Amazon Virtual Private Cloud (Amazon VPC) feature enables users to connect two VPCs together?

A. Amazon VPC endpoints

B. Amazon Elastic Compute Cloud (Amazon EC2) ClassicLink

C. Amazon VPC peering

D. AWS Direct Connect

Answer: C. Amazon VPC peering

36. Which benefit of the AWS Cloud supports matching the supply of resources with changing workload demands?

A. Security

B. Reliability

C. Elasticity

D. High availability

Answer: C. Elasticity

36. What is the total amount of storage offered by Amazon S3?
    A. 100 MB
    B. 5 GB OC
    C. 5 TB
    D. Unlimited
Answer: C. 5 TB

37. Which AWS service can be used to turn text into life-like speech?
    A. Amazon Polly
    B. Amazon Transcribe
    C. Amazon Rekognition
    D. Amazon Lex
Answer: A. Amazon Polly

38. Which AWS services provide a user with connectivity between the AWS Cloud and on-premises resources? (Choose two.)
    A. AWS VPN
    B. Amazon Connect
    C. Amazon Cognito
    D. AWS Direct Connect
    E. AWS Managed Services
Answer: A. AWS VPN, D. AWS Direct Connect

39. Which AWS service should a cloud practitioner use to identify security vulnerabilities of an AWS account?

A. AWS Secrets Manager

B. Amazon Cognito

C. Amazon Macie

D. AWS Trusted Advisor

Answer: D. AWS Trusted Advisor

40. Which of the following Amazon EC2 pricing models allows customers to use existing server-bound software licenses?

A. Spot instances

B. Reserved instances

C. Dedicated Hosts

D. On-Demand Instances

Answer: C. Dedicated Hosts

41. What time-savings advantage is offered with the use of Amazon Rekognition?

A. Amazon Rekognition provides automatic watermarking of images.

B. Amazon Rekognition provides automatic detection of objects appearing in pictures.

C. Amazon Rekognition provides the ability to resize millions of mages automatically.

D. Amazon Rekognition uses Amazon Mechanical Turk to allow humans to bid on object detection jobs.

Answer: B. Amazon Rekognition provides automatic detection of objects appearing in pictures.

42. A Cloud Practitioner needs to store data for 7 years to meet regulatory requirements. Which AWS service will meet this requirement at the LOWEST cost?

    A. Amazon S3

    B. AWS Snowball

    C. Amazon Redshift

    D. Amazon S3 Glacier

Answer: D. Amazon S3 Glacier

43. A company has distributed its workload on both the AWS Cloud and some on-premises servers. What type of architecture is this?

    A. Virtual private network

    B. Virtual private cloud

    C. Hybrid cloud

    D. Private cloud

Answer: C. Hybrid cloud

44. Which service provides a hybrid storage service that enables on-premises applications to seamlessly use cloud storage?

    A. Amazon Glacier

    B. AWS Snowball

    C. AWS Storage Gateway

    D. Amazon Elastic Block Storage

Answer: C. AWS Storage Gateway

45. What TWO services/features are required to have highly available and fault tolerant architecture in AWS? Choose the 2 Correct answers:

    A. Elastic Load Balancer

    B. CloudFront

    C. ElastiCache

    D. Auto Scaling

Answer: A. Elastic Load Balancer, D. Auto Scaling

46. What AWS storage class should be used for long-term, archival storage? Choose the Correct

    A. Glacier

    B. Long-Term

    C. Standard

    D. Infrequent Access

Answer: A. Glacier

47. What are the benefits of DynamoDB? (Select all that apply) Choose the 3 Correct answers:

    A. Supports multiple known NoSQL database engines like MariaDB and Oracle NoSQL.

    B. Automatic scaling of throughput capacity.

    C. Single-digit millisecond latency.

    D. Supports both document and key-value store data mode

Answer: B C D

48. What best describes what AWS is?

    A. AWS is an online retailer

    B. AWS is the cloud.

    C. AWS is a cloud services provider.

    D. None of the above

Answer: C. AWS is a cloud services provider.

49. What is one benefit AND one drawback of buying a reserved EC2 instance? (Select two) Choose the 2 Correct answers:

    A. You can terminate the instance at any time without any further pricing commitment.

    B. Reserved instances can be purchased as a significant discount over on-demand instances.

    C. You can potentially save a lot of money by placing a lower "bid" price.

    D. You are locked in to either a one- or three-year pricing commitment

Answer: B D

50. John is working with a large data set, and he needs to import it into a relational database service. What AWS service will meet his needs?

    A. RDS

    B. Redshift

    C. NoSQL

    D. DynamoDB

Answer: A. RDS

51. Jeff is building a web application on AWS. He wants to make sure his application is highly available to his customers. What infrastructure components of the AWS cloud allow Jeff to accomplish this goal? (Select all that apply) Choose the 2 Correct answers:

    A. Availability Zones

    B. Regional Zones

    C. Regions

    D. Data Locations

Answer: A C

52. What is the most common type of storage used for EC2 instances?

    A. Elastic File System (EFS)

    B. EC2 Hard Drives

    C. Elastic Block Store (EBS)

    D. Magnetic Drive (MD)

Answer: C. Elastic Block Store (EBS)

53. What are the benefits of AWS's Relational Database Service (RDS)? (Select all that apply) Choose the 3 Correct answers:

    A. Resizable capacity

    B. Automated patches and backups

    C. Cost-efficient

    D. None of the above

Answer: A B C

54. Thomas is managing the access rights and credentials for all the employees that have access to his company's AWS account. This morning, his was notified that some of these accounts may have been compromised, and he now needs to change the password policy and re-generate a new password for all users. What AWS service does Thomas need to use in order to accomplish this?

    A. Policy and Access Management

    B. Elastic Cloud Compute

    C. Access Management

    D. None of the above

Answer: D – IAM (Identity and Access Management is required here)

55. You notice that five of your 10 S3 buckets are no longer available in your account, and you assume that they have been deleted. You are unsure who may have deleted them, and no one is taking responsibility. What should you do to investigate and find out who deleted the S3 buckets?

    A. Look at the S3 logs.

    B. Look at the CloudTrail logs.

    C. Look at the CloudWatch Logs.

    D. Look at the SNS log

Answer: B. Look at the CloudTrail logs.

56. What acts as an address (like a mailing address) for a web server located on a network?

    A. DNS Server

    B. IP Address

    C. Common language domain name

    D. None of the above

Answer: B. IP Address

57. Derek is running a web application and is noticing that he is paying for way more server capacity then is required. What AWS feature should Derek set up and configure to ensure that his application is automatically adding/removing server capacity to keep in line with the required demand?

    A. Auto Scaling

    B. Elastic Server Scaling

    C. Elastic Load Balancing

    D. Auto Sizing

Answer: A. Auto Scaling

58. What is the purpose of AWS's Route 53 service? (Select all that apply) Choose the 2 Correct answers:

    A. Content Caching

    B. Database Management

    C. Domain Registration

    D. Domain Name System (DNS) service

Answer: C D

59. What AWS service allows you to have your own private network in the AWS cloud?

    A. Virtual Private Network (VPN)

    B. Virtual Private Cloud (VPC)

    C. Virtual Cloud Network (VCN)

    D. None of the above

Answer: B. Virtual Private Cloud (VPC)

60. David is managing a web application running on dozens of EC2 servers. He is worried that if something goes wrong with one of the servers, he will not know about it in a timely manner. What solution could you offer to help him keep updated on the status of his servers?

A. Configure each EC2 instance with a custom script to email David when any issues occur.

B. Configure RDS notifications based on CloudWatch EC2 metric alarms.

C. Enable CloudTrail to log and report any issues that occur with the EC2 instances.

D. Configure SNS notifications based on CloudWatch EC2 metric alarm

Answer: D. Configure SNS notifications based on CloudWatch EC2 metric alarm

61. What is the purpose of a DNS server?
A. To serve web application content.
B. To convert common language domain names to IP addresses.
C. To convert IP addresses to common language domain names.
D. To act as an internet search engine

Answer: B. To convert common language domain names to IP addresses.

62. Mike is setting up the infrastructure for a web application that requires three EC2 instances to handle the expected demand. However, when testing the application, Mike find that all traffic to the application is being routed to only one of the servers. What AWS feature should he add to his application in order to have traffic evenly distributed between all three servers?
A. Elastic Load Balancer
B. Auto Scaling
C. Route 53
D. CloudFront

Answer: A. Elastic Load Balancer

63. What are the TWO main security layers (firewalls) used inside a VPC? Choose the 2 Correct answers:

    A. NetProtect

    B. Network Access Control List

    C. Security Group

    D. Security List

Answer: B C

64. What best describes the concept of a virtual private cloud?

    A. A private section of AWS in which you control what resources are placed inside.

    B. A collection of data centers.

    C. A shared section of AWS between you and other AWS account holders.

    D. A private section of AWS in which you control what resources are placed inside and who can access those resources.

Answer: D. A private section of AWS in which you control what resources are placed inside and who can access those resources.

65. In S3, what is a file that you upload called?

    A. Static File

    B. Bucket

    C. Folder

    D. Object

Answer: D. Object

66. What AWS database service is used for data warehousing of petabytes of data?

    A. RDS

    B. Elasticache

    C. Redshift

    D. DynamoDB

Answer: C. Redshift

67. What is AWS's relational database service?

    A. Redshift

    B. DymamoDB

    C. ElastiCache

    D. RDS

Answer: D. RDS

68. What is the major difference between AWS's RDS and DynamoDB database services?

    A. RDS offers NoSQL database options, and DynamoDB offers SQL database options.

    B. RDS offers on SQL database option, and DynamoDB offers many NoSQL database options.

    C. RDS offers SQL database options, and DynamoDB offers a NoSQL database option.

    D. None of the above

Answer: C. RDS offers SQL database options, and DynamoDB offers a NoSQL database option.

69. Under what circumstances would you choose to use the AWS service CloudTrail

    A. When you want to collect and view resource metrics.

    B. When you want to log what actions various IAM users are taking in your AWS account.

    C. When you want a serverless compute platform.

    D. When you want to send SMS notificaitions based on events that occur in your account

Answer: B. When you want to log what actions various IAM users are taking in your AWS account.

70. Which of the following are AWS Support Plans? (Select all that apply) Choose the 3 Correct answers:

    A. Enterprise

    B. Expert

    C. Basic

    D. Business

Answer: A C D

71. What does TCO stand for

    A. Tally of Cost Ownership

    B. Total Continual Ownership

    C. The Cost of Ownership

    D. None of the above

Answer: D. None of the above. Explanation: TCO stand for Total Cost of Ownership

72. Which of the following are AWS security best practices for using AWS Identity and Access Management (IAM) to manage an AWS account root user? (Choose two.)

    A. Set up multi-factor authentication (MFA) for the root user.

    B. Remove all IAM policies from the root user.

    C. Delete the root user access keys.

    D. Use the root user for daily tasks.

    E. Assign a read-only access policy to the root use

Answer: A C

73. Service control policies (SCPs) manage permissions for which of the following?

    A. Availability Zones

    B. AWS Regions

    C. AWS Organizations

    D. Edge location

Answer: C. AWS Organizations

74. A database administrator is trying to determine who deleted a critical Amazon Redshift cluster. Which AWS service helps with monitoring and retaining this type of account activity?

    A. AWS CloudTrail

    B. AWS Organizations

    C. AWS Identity and Access Management (IAM)

    D. AWS Trusted Advisor

Answer: A. AWS CloudTrail

75. Which pillar of the AWS Well-Architected Framework includes the AWS shared responsibility model?

    A. Operational excellence

    B. Performance efficiency

    C. Reliability

    D. Security

Answer: D. Security

76. A company runs its business-critical web application on Amazon Elastic Container Service (Amazon ECS) and Amazon DynamoDB. The workload spikes up to 10 times the normal workload multiple times during the day. Which AWS Cloud feature enables the company to meet these changes in demand?

    A. Agility

    B. Global reach

    C. Scalability

    D. Security

Answer: C. Scalability

77. A company's traffic logs show that IP addresses owned by AWS are being used in an attempt to flood ports on system resources. To whom should the cloud practitioner report this issue?

    A. AWS Professional Services

    B. AWS Abuse team

    C. AWS Partner Network (APN)

    D. AWS technical account manager (TAM)

Answer: B. AWS Abuse team

78. Which AWS services can be used as infrastructure automation tools? (Select TWO.)

    A. AWS CloudFormation

    B. Amazon CloudFront

    C. AWS Batch

    D. AWS OpsWorks

    E. Amazon QuickSight

Answer: A D

79. What technology enables compute capacity to adjust as loads change?

    A. Load Balancing

    B Automatic failover

    C Round Robin

    D Auto Scaling

Answer: D Auto Scaling

80. How can a company separate costs for storage, Amazon EC2, Amazon S3, and other AWS services by department?

    A. Add department specific tags to each res

    B. Create separate VPC for each dept

    C. create separate AWS account for each dept

    D. Use AWS Organizations

Answer: C. create separate AWS account for each dept

81. Which AWS Support package includes access to architectural and operational assessments, as well as 24/7 email, online chat, and phone support from Senior Cloud Support Engineers?

    A. Basic
    B. Business
    C. Developer
    D. Enterprise
Answer: D. Enterprise

82. Which AWS service provides on-demand downloads of AWS security and compliance reports?
    A. Aws Directory Service
    B. AWS Artifact
    C. Aws Trusted Advisor
    D. Amazon Inspector
Answer: A. Aws Directory Service

83. Which Amazon EC2 pricing model provides the MOST cost savings for an always-up, right-sized database server running for a project that will last 1 year?
    A. On-Demand Instances
    B. Standard Reserved Instances
    C. Spot Instances
    D. Convertible Reserved Instances
Answer: D. Convertible Reserved Instances

84. Which feature enables fast, easy, and secure transfers of files over long distances between a client and an Amazon S3 bucket?
    A. S3 Static Website
    B. S3 Copy
    C. Multi part upload
    D. S3 Transfer Acceleration
Answer: D. S3 Transfer Acceleration

85. An Amazon EC2 instance previously used for development is inaccessible and no longer appears in the AWS Management Console. Which AWS service should be used to determine what action made this EC2 instance inaccessible?

A. Amazon CloudWatch Logs

B. AWS Security Hub

C. Amazon Inspector

D. AWS CloudTrail

Answer: D. AWS CloudTrail

86. Which AWS service is a highly available and scalable DNS web service?

A. Amazon VPC

B. Amazon CloudFront

C. Amazon Route 53

D. Amazon Connect

Answer: C. Amazon Route 53

87. A company is moving its office and must establish an encrypted connection to AWS. Which AWS service will help meet this requirement?

A. AWS VPN

B. Amazon Route 53

C. Amazon API Gateway

D. Amazon Connect

Answer: A. AWS VPN

88. Which statement explains the benefit of agility in the AWS Cloud?

A. Agility gives users the ability to host applications in multiple AWS Regions around the world. B. Agility gives users the ability to pay upfront to reduce cost.

C. Agility provides customizable physical hardware at the lowest possible cost.

D. Agility provides the means for users to provision resources in minutes

Answer: D. Agility provides the means for users to provision resources in minutes

89. Which of the following are user authentication services managed by AWS? (Choose two.)

    A. Amazon Cognito
    B. AWS Lambda
    C. AWS License Manager
    D. AWS Identity and Access Management (IAM)

Answer: A D

90. Which AWS service or tool helps identify underutilized Amazon EC2 instances and idle Amazon RDS DB instances at no additional charge?
    A. Cost Explorer
    B. AWS Budgets
    C. AWS Organizations
    D. AWS Trusted Advisor

Answer: D. AWS Trusted Advisor

91. Which of the following are customer responsibilities under the AWS shared responsibility model? (Choose two.)

    A. Physical security of AWS facilities
    B. Configuration of security groups
    C. Encryption of customer data on AWS
    D. Management of AWS Lambda infrastructure
    E. Management of network throughput of each AWS Region

Answer: D E

92. A user should contact the AWS Abuse team to report which situations? (Choose two.)

A. A DDoS attack is being made on an AWS resource.

B. A SQL injection attack is being made from an IP address that is not an AWS address.

C. AWS resources are being used to host objectionable or illegal content.

D. A company's resources are being used in a way that is inconsistent with corporate policy.

E. A company is receiving HTTPS requests on a web server that I s serving HTTP.

Answer: A C

93. A company uses Amazon DynamoDB in its AWS Cloud architecture. According to the AWS shared responsibility model, which of the following are responsibilities of the company? (Choose two.)

A. Operating system patching and upgrades

B. Application of appropriate permissions with IAM tools

C. Configuration of data encryption options

D. Creation of DynamoDB endpoints

E. Infrastructure provisioning and maintenance

Answer: B D

94. What should a user do to deploy an application in geographically separate locations?

A. Deploy the application in different placement groups.

B. Deploy the application to a VPC.

C. Deploy the application to multiple AWS Regions

D. Deploy the application by using Amazon CloudFront

Answer: C. Deploy the application to multiple AWS Regions

95. A company wants to rightsize its infrastructure to control costs. At which points should the company rightsize? (Choose two.)

A. Rightsize before a migration occurs to the cloud.

B. Rightsize continuously after the cloud onboarding process.

C. Rightsize when AWS Support calls and explains that rightsizing is needed.

D. Rightsize when seasonal workloads are at their peak.

E. Rightsize after purchasing all Reserved Instances.

Answer: D   E

96. Which tasks should a user perform if the user suspects that an AWS account has been compromised? (Choose two.)

A. Remove any multi-factor authentication (MFA) tokens.

B. Rotate and delete all AWS access keys.

C. Move resources to a different AWS Region.

D. Delete AWS CloudTrail resources.

E. Contact AWS Support

Answer: B E

97. A company needs a content delivery network that provides secure delivery of data, videos, applications, and APIs to users globally with low latency and high transfer speed. Which AWS service meets these requirements?

A. Amazon CloudFront

B. Elastic Load Balancing

C. Amazon S3

D. Amazon Elastic Transcoder

Answer: A. Amazon CloudFront

98. Which AWS Cloud benefit is shown by an architecture's ability to withstand failures with minimal downtime?

    A. Agility
    B. Elasticity
    C. Scalability
    D. High availability

Answer: D. High availability

99. A company is moving its development and test environments to AWS to increase agility and reduce cost. Because these are not production workloads and the servers are not fully utilized, occasional unavailability is acceptable. What is the MOST cost-effective Amazon EC2 pricing model that will meet these requirements?

    A. Reserved Instances
    B. On-Demand Instances
    C. Spot Instances
    D. Dedicated Instances

Answer: C. Spot Instances

100. Which guidelines are key AWS architectural design principles? (Choose two.)

    A. Design for fixed resources.
    B. Build scalable architectures.
    C. Use tightly coupled components.
    D. Use managed services when possible.
    E. Design for human interaction

Answer: B D

101. What is the LEAST expensive AWS Support plan that provides 24-hour access to AWS customer service and AWS communities?

    A. AWS Enterprise Support
    B. AWS Business Support
    C. AWS Developer Support
    D. AWS Basic Support

Answer: D. AWS Basic Support

102. A company with AWS Enterprise Support has questions about its consolidated bill. Which AWS service, feature, or tool should the company use for assistance?

    A. AWS Pricing Calculator

    B. AWS Concierge Support

    C. AWS Trusted Advisor

    D. AWS Budget

Answer: C. AWS Trusted Advisor

103. A company needs to perform a one-time migration of 40TB of data from its on-premises storage servers to Amazon S3. The transfer must happen as quickly as possible while keeping costs to a minimum. The company has 100 Mbps internet connectivity. Which AWS service will meet these requirements?

    A. AWS Snowball

    B. AWS Direct Connect

    C. AWS Storage Gateway

    D. Amazon S3 Transfer Acceleration

Answer: A. AWS Snowball

104. A company uses Amazon S3 buckets. One of the company's departments enabled S3 Cross-Region Replication for those buckets to meet new requirements. The company's bill for that month was larger than usual. Which AWS service or feature can the company use to confirm that the cost increase was caused by the data replication?

    A. Consolidated billing

    B. Cost Explorer

    C. AWS Pricing Calculator

    D. AWS Trusted Advisor

Answer: A. Consolidated billing

105. Which design principles of the AWS Well-Architected Framework help increase reliability? (Select TWO.)

    A. Automatically recovers from failure

    B. Enable traceability.

    C. Scale horizontally to increase workload availability.

    D. Automate security best practices

    E. Keep people away from data

Answer: A C

106. Which AWS service provides a report that enables users to assess AWS infrastructure compliance?

    A. AWS Certificate Manager (ACM)

    B. Amazon DocumentDB (with MongoDB compatibility)

    C. AWS Artifact

    D. AWS Trusted Advisor

Answer: C. AWS Artifact

107. Which AWS service provides the ability to quickly run one-time queries on data in Amazon S3?

    A. Amazon EMR

    B. Amazon DynamoDB

    C. Amazon Redshift

    D. Amazon Athena

Answer: D. Amazon Athena

108. A company with an AWS Business Support plan wants to identify Amazon EC2 Reserved that are scheduled to expire. Which AWS service or feature can the company use to accomplish this goal?

    A. AWS Personal Health Dashboard

    B. Elastic Load Balancing health checks

    C. AWS Trusted Advisor

    D. EC2 instance status checks

Answer: C. AWS Trusted Advisor

109. To optimize costs and resource usage, a company needs to monitor the operations health of its entire system of AWS Cloud resources. Which AWS service will meet these requirements?

A. AWS Organizations

B. Amazon CloudWatch

C. AWS CloudTrail

D. AWS Config

Answer: B. Amazon CloudWatch

110. Which AWS service can help a company detect an outage of its website servers and redirect users to alternate servers?

A. Amazon CloudFront

B. Amazon GuardDuty

C. Amazon Route 53

D. AWS Trusted Advisor

Answer: C. Amazon Route 53

111. What is the recommended method to request penetration testing on AWS resources?

A. Open a support case.

B. Fill out the Penetration Testing Request Form

C. Request a penctration tcst from your technical account manager.

D. Contact your AWS sales representative.

Answer: B. Fill out the Penetration Testing Request Form

112. A company wants to ensure that two Amazon EC2 instances are in separate data centers with minimal communication latency between the data centers. How can the company meet this requirement?

    A. Place the EC2 instances in two separate AWS Regions connected with a VPC peering connection.

    B. Place the EC2 instances in two separate Availability Zones within the same AWS Region.

    C. Place one EC2 instance on premises and the other in an AWS Region Then connect them by using an AWS VPN connection.

    D. Place both EC2 instances in a placement group for dedicated bandwidth

Answer: B. Place the EC2 instances in two separate Availability Zones within the same AWS Region.

113. A user has a stateful workload that will run on Amazon EC2 for the next 3 years. What is the MOST cost-effective pricing model for this workload?

    A. On-Demand Instances

    B. Reserved Instances

    C. Dedicated Instances

    D. Spot Instances

Answer: B. Reserved Instances

114. When comparing AWS with on-premises Total Cost of Ownership (TCO), what costs are included?

    A. Data center security

    B. Business analysis

    C. Project management

    D. Operating system administration

Answer: A. Data center security

115. Which AWS service is suitable for an event driven workload?

    A. Amazon EC2

    B. AWS Elastic Beanstalk

    C. AWS Lambda

    D. Amazon Lumberyard

Answer: B. AWS Elastic Beanstalk

116. Which of the following is the responsibility of AWS?

    A. Setting up AWS Identity and Access Management (IAM) users and groups

    B. Physically destroying storage media at end-of-life

    C. Patching guest operating systems

    D. Configuring security settings on Amazon EC2 instances

Answer: B. Physically destroying storage media at end-of-life

117. A company is considering moving its on-premises data center to AWS. What factors should be included in doing a Total Cost of Ownership (TCO) analysis? (Choose two.)

    A. Amazon EC2 instance availability

    B. Power consumption of the data center

    C. Labor costs to replace old servers

    D. Application developer time

    E. Database engine capacity

Answer: B C

118. Where can users find a catalog of AWS-recognized providers of third-party security solutions?

    A. AWS Service Catalog

    B. AWS Marketplace

    C. AWS Quick Start OD

    D. AWS CodeDeploy

Answer: A. AWS Service Catalog

119. What is an example of high availability in the AWS Cloud?

    A. Consulting AWS technical support at any time day or night

    B. Ensuring an application remains accessible, even if a resource fails

    C. Making any AWS service available for use by paying on demand

    D. Deploying in any part of the world using AWS Regions

Answer: B. Ensuring an application remains accessible, even if a resource fails

120. Which of the following is a component of the AWS Global Infrastructure?

    A. Amazon Alexa

    B. AWS Regions

    C. Amazon Lightsail

    D. AWS Organizations

Answer: B. AWS Regions

121. Which AWS service will provide a way to generate encryption keys that can be used to encrypt data? (Select TWO.)

    A. Amazon Macie

    B. AWS Certificate Manager

    C. AWS Key Management Service (AWS KMS)

    D. AWS Secrets Manager

    E. AWS CloudHSM

Answer: C E

122. According to the AWS shared responsibility model, which of the following tasks are AWS responsibilities? (Select TWO.)

    A. The physical security of AWS facilities.

    B. Encrypting customer data.

    C. Patching and updating the hypervisor.

    D. Patching operating systems on Amazon EC2.

    E. Defining network firewalls inside the VPC.

Answer: A C

123. Which AWS service or tool simplifies the creation, maintenance, validation, sharing and deployment of Linux or Windows Server templates for use with Amazon EC2 and on premises VMs?

    A. AWS CodePipeline

    B. Amazon EC2 Image Builder

    C. AWS CloudFormation

    D. Amazon EC2 Amazon Machine Image (AMI)

Answer: B. Amazon EC2 Image Builder

124. Which service enables risk auditing by continuously monitoring and logging account activity, including user actions in the AWS Management Console and AWS SDKs?

    A. Amazon CloudWatch

    B. AWS CloudTrail

    C. AWS Config

    D. AWS Health

Answer: B. AWS CloudTrail

125. An administrator observed that multiple AWS resources were deleted yesterday. Which AWS service will help identify the cause and determine which user deleted the resources?

    A. AWS CloudTrail

    B. Amazon Inspector

    C. Amazon GuardDuty

    D. AWS Trusted Advisor

Answer: B. Amazon Inspector

126. Which statement is true about AWS global infrastructure

    A. Availability Zones can span multiple AWS Regions.

    B. A VPC can have different subnets in different AWS Regions.

    C. AWS Regions consist of multiple Availability Zones.

    D. A single subnet can span multiple Availability Zones.

Answer: C. AWS Regions consist of multiple Availability Zones.

127. An application is receiving SQL injection attacks from multiple external resources. Which AWS service or feature can help automate mitigation against these attacks?

    A. AWS WAF

    B. Security groups

    C. Elastic Load Balancer

    D. Network ACL

Answer: A. AWS WAF – Web Application Firewall

128. Which Amazon EC2 pricing option is best suited for applications with short-term, spiky, or unpredictable workloads that cannot be interrupted?

    A. Spot Instances

    B. Dedicated Hosts

    C. On-Demand Instances

    D. Reserved Instances

Answer: C. On-Demand Instances

129. Which AWS service should be used for long-term, low-cost storage of data backups?

    A. Amazon RDS

    B. Amazon Glacier

    C. AWS Snowball

    D. AWS EBS

Answer: B. Amazon Glacier

130. Which of the following are benefits of using the AWS Cloud? (Select TWO)

    A. Fault tolerance

    B. Total control over underlying infrastructure

    C. Fast provisioning of IT resources

    D. Outsourcing all application coding to AWS

    E. Ability to go global quickly

Answer: A B

131. What exclusive benefit is provided to users with Enterprise Support?
    A. Access to a Technical Project Manager
    B. Access to a Technical Account Manager
    C. Access to a Cloud Support Engineer
    D. Access to a Solutions Architect
Answer: C. Access to a Cloud Support Engineer

132. Which of the following is a correct relationship between regions, Availability Zones, and edge locations?
    A. Data centers contain regions.
    B. Regions contain Availability Zones.
    C. Availability Zones contain edge locations.
    D. Edge locations contain regions.
Answer: B. Regions contain Availability Zones.

133. A director has been tasked with investigating hybrid cloud architecture. The company currently accesses AWS over the public internet. Which service will facilitate private hybrid connectivity?
    A. Amazon Virtual Private Cloud (Amazon VPC) NAT Gateway
    B. AWS Direct Connect
    C. Amazon Simple Storage Service (Amazon S3) Transfer Acceleration
    D. AWS Web Application Firewall (AWS WAF)
Answer: B. AWS Direct Connect

134. A company wants to use an AWS service to continuously monitor the health of its application endpoints based on proximity to application users. The company also needs to route traffic to healthy regional endpoints and to improve application availability and performance. Which service will meet these requirements?
    A. Amazon Inspector
    B. Amazon CloudWatch
    C. AWS Global Accelerator
    D. AWS Cloud Formation
Answer: C. AWS Global Accelerator

135. Does DynamoDB support in-place atomic updates?

    A. Yes

    B. No

    C. It does support in-place non0-atomic updates

    D. It is not defined

Answer: A. Yes

136. Much of your company's data does not need to be accessed often, and can take several hours for retrieval time, so it's stored on Amazon Glacier. However someone within your organization has expressed concerns that his data is more sensitive than the other data, and is wondering whether the high level of encryption that he knows is on S3 is also used on the much cheaper Glacier service. Which of the following statements would be most applicable in regard to this concern?

    A. There is no encryption on Amazon Glacier, that's why it is cheaper.

    B. Amazon Glacier automatically encrypts the data using AES-128 a lesser encryption method than Amazon S3 but you can change it to AES-256 if you are willing to pay more.

    C. Amazon Glacier automatically encrypts the data using AES-256, the same as Amazon S3.

    D. Amazon Glacier automatically encrypts the data using AES-128 a lesser encryption mcthod than Amazon S3.

Answer: C. Amazon Glacier automatically encrypts the data using AES-256, the same as Amazon S3.

137. You need to set up a complex network infrastructure for your organization that will be reasonably easy to deploy, replicate, control, and track changes on. Which AWS service would be best to use to help you accomplish this?

    A. AWS Import/Export

    B. AWS CloudFormation

    C. Amazon Route 53

    D. Amazon CIoudWatch

Answer: B. AWS CloudFormation

138. The use of what AWS feature or service allows companies to track and categorize spending on a detailed level?

    A. Cost allocation tags

    B. Consolidated billing

    C. AWS Budgets

    D. AWS Marketplace

Answer: C. AWS Budgets

139. Which service stores objects, provides real-time access to those objects, and offers versioning and lifecycle capabilities?

    A. Amazon Glacier

    B. AWS Storage Gateway

    C. Amazon S3

    D. Amazon EBS

Answer: C. Amazon S3

140. What AWS team assists customers with accelerating cloud adoption through paid engagements in any of several specialty practice areas?

    A. AWS Enterprise Support

    B. AWS Solutions Architects

    C. AWS Professional Services

    D. AWS Account Managers

Answer: C. AWS Professional Services

141. A customer would like to design and build a new workload on AWS Cloud but does not have the AWSrelated software technical expertise in-house. Which of the following AWS programs can a customer take advantage of to achieve that outcome?

    A. AWS Partner Network Technology Partners

    B. AWS Marketplace

    C. AWS Partner Network Consulting Partners

    D. AWS Service Catalog

Answer: C. AWS Partner Network Consulting Partners

142. Distributing workloads across multiple Availability Zones supports which cloud architecture design principle?

    A. Implement automation.

    B. Design for agility.

    C. Design for failure.

    D. Implement elasticity.

Answer: C. Design for failure.

143. Which AWS services can host a Microsoft SQL Server database? (Choose two.)

    A. Amazon EC2

    B. Amazon Relational Database Service (Amazon RDS)

    C. Amazon Aurora

    D. Amazon Redshift

    E. Amazon S3

Answer: A B

144. Which of the following inspects AWS environments to find opportunities that can save money for users and also improve system performance?

    A. AWS Cost Explorer

    B. AWS Trusted Advisor

    C. Consolidated billing

    D. Detailed billing

Answer: B. AWS Trusted Advisor

145. Which of the following Amazon EC2 pricing models allow customers to use existing server-bound software licenses?

    A. Spot Instances

    B. Reserved Instances

    C. Dedicated Hosts

    D. On-Demand Instances

Answer: C. Dedicated Hosts

146. Which AWS characteristics make AWS cost effective for a workload with dynamic user demand? (Choose two.)
    A. High availability
    B. Shared security model
    C. Elasticity
    D. Pay-as-you-go pricing
    E. Reliability

Answer: C D

147. Which of the following are characteristics of Amazon S3? (Choose two.)
    A. A global file system
    B. An object store
    C. A local file store
    D. A network file system
    E. A durable storage system

Answer: B E

148. Which services can be used across hybrid AWS Cloud architectures? (Choose two.)
    A. Amazon Route 53
    B. Virtual Private Gateway
    C. Classic Load Balancer
    D. Auto Scaling
    E. Amazon CloudWatch default metric

Answer: A B

149. What costs are included when comparing AWS Total Cost of Ownership (TCO) with on-premises TCO?
    A. Project management
    B. Antivirus software licensing
    C. Data center security
    D. Software development

Answer: C. Data center security

150. A company is considering using AWS for a self-hosted database that requires a nightly shutdown for maintenance and cost-saving purposes. Which service should the company use?

    A. Amazon Redshift

    B. Amazon DynamoDB

    C. Amazon Elastic Compute Cloud (Amazon EC2) with Amazon EC2 instance store

    D. Amazon EC2 with Amazon Elastic Block Store (Amazon EBS)

Answer: D. Amazon EC2 with Amazon Elastic Block Store (Amazon EBS)

151. Which AWS tools assist with estimating costs? (Choose three.)

    A. Detailed billing report

    B. Cost allocation tags

    C. AWS Simple Monthly Calculator

    D. AWS Total Cost of Ownership (TCO) Calculator

    E. Cost Estimator

Answer: B C D

152. Which of the following are advantages of AWS consolidated billing? (Choose two.)

    A. The ability to receive one bill for multiple accounts

    B. Service limits increasing by default in all accounts

    C. A fixed discount on the monthly bill

    D. Potential volume discounts, as usage in all accounts is combined

    E. The automatic extension of the master account's AWS support plan to all accounts

Answer: A D

153. Which of the following Reserved Instance (RI) pricing models provides the highest average savings compared to On-Demand pricing.

    A. One-year, No Upfront, Standard RI pricing

    B. One-year, All Upfront, Convertible RI pricing

    C. Three-year, All Upfront, Standard RI pricing

    D. Three-year, No Upfront, Convertible RI pricing

Answer: C. Three-year, All Upfront, Standard RI pricing

154. Compared with costs in traditional and virtualized data centers, AWS has:

A. greater variable costs and greater upfront costs.

B. fixed usage costs and lower upfront costs.

C. lower variable costs and greater upfront costs.

D. lower variable costs and lower upfront costs.

Answer: D. lower variable costs and lower upfront costs.

155. A characteristic of edge locations is that they:

A. host Amazon EC2 instances closer to users.

B. help lower latency and improve performance for users.

C. cache frequently changing data without reaching the origin server.

D. refresh data changes daily

Answer: C. cache frequently changing data without reaching the origin server.

156. Which of the following can limit Amazon Storage Service (Amazon S3) bucket access to specific users?

A. A public and private key-pair

B. Amazon Inspector

C. AWS Identity and Access Management (IAM) policies

D. Security Groups

Answer: C. AWS Identity and Access Management (IAM) policies

157. Which of the following security-related actions are available at no cost?

A. Calling AWS Support

B. Contacting AWS Professional Services to request a workshop

C. Accessing forums, blogs, and whitepapers

D. Attending AWS classes at a local university

Answer: C. Accessing forums, blogs, and whitepapers

158. Which of the Reserved Instance (RI) pricing models can change the attributes of the RI as long as the exchange results in the creation of RIs of equal or greater value?

    A. Dedicated RIs

    B. Scheduled RIs

    C. Convertible RIs

    D. Standard RIs

Answer: C. Convertible RIs

159. Which AWS feature will reduce the customer's total cost of ownership (TCO)?

    A. Shared responsibility security model

    B. Single tenancy

    C. Elastic computing

    D. Encryption

Answer: C. Elastic computing

160. Which of the following services will automatically scale with an expected increase in web traffic?

    A. AWS CodePipeline

    B. Elastic Load Balancing

    C. Amazon EBS

    D. AWS Direct Connect

Answer: B. Elastic Load Balancing

161. Under the AWS shared responsibility model, which of the following activities are the customer's responsibility? (Choose two.)

    A. Patching operating system components for Amazon Relational Database Server (Amazon RDS) B. Encrypting data on the client-side

    C. Training the data center staff

    D. Configuring Network Access Control Lists (ACL)

    E. Maintaining environmental controls within a data center

Answer: B D

162. Which is a recommended pattern for designing a highly available architecture on AWS?

    A. Ensure that components have low-latency network connectivity.

    B. Run enough Amazon EC2 instances to operate at peak load.

    C. Ensure that the application is designed to accommodate failure of any single component.

    D. Use a monolithic application that handles all operations.

Answer: C. Ensure that the application is designed to accommodate failure of any single component.

163. According to best practices, how should an application be designed to run in the AWS Cloud?

    A. Use tightly coupled components.

    B. Use loosely coupled components.

    C. Use infrequently coupled components.

    D. Use frequently coupled components.

Answer: B. Use loosely coupled components.

164. AWS supports which of the following methods to add security to Identity and Access Management (IAM) users? (Choose two.)

    A. Implementing Amazon Rekognition

    B. Using AWS Shield-protected resources

    C. Blocking access with Security Groups

    D. Using Multi-Factor Authentication (MFA)

    E. Enforcing password strength and expiration

Answer: D E

165. Which AWS services should be used for read/write of constantly changing data? (Choose two.)

    A. Amazon Glacier

    B. Amazon RDS

    C. AWS Snowball

    D. Amazon Redshift

    E. Amazon EFS

Answer: B E

166. What is one of the advantages of the Amazon Relational Database Service (Amazon RDS)?

    A. It simplifies relational database administration tasks.

    B. It provides 99.99999999999% reliability and durability.

    C. It automatically scales databases for loads.

    D. It enables users to dynamically adjust CPU and RAM resources.

Answer: A. It simplifies relational database administration tasks.

167. A customer needs to run a MySQL database that easily scales. Which AWS service should they use?

    A. Amazon Aurora

    B. Amazon Redshift

    C. Amazon DynamoDB

    D. Amazon ElastiCache

Answer: A. Amazon Aurora

168. Which of the following components of the AWS Global Infrastructure consists of one or more discrete data centers interconnected through low latency links?

    A. Availability Zone

    B. Edge location

    C. Region

    D. Private networking

Answer: C. Region

169. Which of the following is a shared control between the customer and AWS?

    A. Providing a key for Amazon S3 client-side encryption

    B. Configuration of an Amazon EC2 instance

    C. Environmental controls of physical AWS data centers

    D. Awareness and training

Answer: D. Awareness and training

170. How many Availability Zones should compute resources be provisioned across to achieve high availability?

    A. A minimum of one
    B. A minimum of two
    C. A minimum of three
    D. A minimum of four or more

Answer: B. A minimum of two

171. One of the advantages to moving infrastructure from an on-premises data center to the AWS Cloud is:

    A. it allows the business to eliminate IT bills
    B. it allows the business to put a server in each customer's data center.
    C. it allows the business to focus on business activities.
    D. it allows the business to leave servers unpatched.

Answer: C. it allows the business to focus on business activities.

172. What is the lowest-cost, durable storage option for retaining database backups for immediate retrieval?

    A. Amazon S3
    B. Amazon Glacier
    C. Amazon EBS
    D. Amazon EC2 Instance Store

Answer: A. Amazon S3

173. Which AWS IAM feature allows developers to access AWS services through the AWS CLI?

    A. API keys
    B. Access keys
    C. User names/Passwords
    D. SSH keys

Answer: B. Access keys

174. Which of the following is a fast and reliable NoSQL database service?

    A. Amazon Redshift

    B. Amazon RDS

    C. Amazon DynamoDB

    D. Amazon S3

Answer: C. Amazon DynamoDB

175. Which service should a customer use to consolidate and centrally manage multiple AWS accounts?

    A. AWS IAM

    B. AWS Organizations

    C. AWS Schema Conversion Tool

    D. AWS Config

Answer: B. AWS Organizations

176. What approach to transcoding a large number of individual video files adheres to AWS architecture principles?

    A. Using many instances in parallel

    B. Using a single large instance during off-peak hours

    C. Using dedicated hardware

    D. Using a large GPU instance type

Answer: A. Using many instances in parallel

177. For which auditing process does AWS have sole responsibility?

    A. AWS IAM policies

    B. Physical security

    C. Amazon S3 bucket policies

    D. AWS CloudTrail Logs

Answer: B. Physical security

178. Which feature of the AWS Cloud will support an international company's requirement for low latency to all of its customers?

A. Fault tolerance

B. Global reach

C. Pay-as-you-go pricing

D. High availability

Answer: B. Global reach

179. Which of the following is the customer's responsibility under the AWS shared responsibility model?

A. Patching underlying infrastructure

B. Physical security

C. Patching Amazon EC2 instances

D. Patching network infrastructure

Answer: C. Patching Amazon EC2 instances

180. A customer is using multiple AWS accounts with separate billing. How can the customer take advantage of volume discounts with minimal impact to the AWS resources?

A. Create one global AWS account and move all AWS resources to that account.

B. Sign up for three years of Reserved Instance pricing up front.

C. Use the consolidated billing feature from AWS Organizations.

D. Sign up for the AWS Enterprise support plan to get volume discounts

Answer: C. Use the consolidated billing feature from AWS Organizations.

181. Which of the following are features of Amazon CloudWatch Logs? (Choose two.)

A. Summaries by Amazon Simple Notification Service (Amazon SNS)

B. Free Amazon Elasticsearch Service analytics

C. Provided at no charge

D. Real-time monitoring

E. Adjustable retention

Answer: D E

182. Which of the following is an AWS managed Domain Name System (DNS) web service?

    A. Amazon Route 53

    B. Amazon Neptune

    C. Amazon SageMaker

    D. Amazon Lightsail

Answer: A. Amazon Route 53

183. A customer is deploying a new application and needs to choose an AWS Region. Which of the following factors could influence the customer's decision? (Choose two.)

    A. Reduced latency to users

    B. The application's presentation in the local language

    C. Data sovereignty compliance

    D. Cooling costs in hotter climates

    E. Proximity to the customer's office for on-site visits

Answer: A C

184. Which storage service can be used as a low-cost option for hosting static websites?

    A. Amazon Glacier

    B. Amazon DynamoDB

    C. Amazon Elastic File System (Amazon EFS)

    D. Amazon Simple Storage Service (Amazon S3)

Answer: D. Amazon Simple Storage Service (Amazon S3)

185. Which Amazon EC2 instance pricing model can provide discounts of up to 90%?

    A. Reserved Instances

    B. On-Demand

    C. Dedicated Hosts

    D. Spot Instances

Answer: D. Spot Instances

186. Which of the following AWS Cloud services can be used to run a customer-managed relational database?

A. Amazon EC2

B. Amazon Route 53

C. Amazon ElastiCache

D. Amazon DynamoDB

Answer: A. Amazon EC2

187. A company is looking for a scalable data warehouse solution. Which of the following AWS solutions would meet the company's needs?

A. Amazon Simple Storage Service (Amazon S3)

B. Amazon DynamoDB

C. Amazon Kinesis

D. Amazon Redshift

Answer: D. Amazon Redshift

188. Which statement best describes Elastic Load Balancing?

A. It translates a domain name into an IP address using DNS.

B. It distributes incoming application traffic across one or more Amazon EC2 instances

C. It collects metrics on connected Amazon EC2 instances.

D. It automatically adjusts the number of Amazon EC2 instances to support incoming traffic.

Answer: B. It distributes incoming application traffic across one or more Amazon EC2 instances

189. Which of the following are valid ways for a customer to interact with AWS services? (Choose two.)

A. Command line interface

B. On-premises

C. Software Development Kits

D. Software-as-a-service

E. Hybrid Correct

Answer: A C

190. Which of the following AWS services can be used to serve large amounts of online video content with the lowest possible latency? (Choose two.)

A. AWS Storage Gateway

B. Amazon S3

C. Amazon Elastic File System (EFS)

D. Amazon Glacier

E. Amazom CloudFront

Answer: B E

191. Web servers running on Amazon EC2 access a legacy application running in a corporate data center. What term would describe this model?

A. Cloud-native

B. Partner network

C. Hybrid architecture

D. Infrastructure as a service

Answer: C. Hybrid architecture

192. What is the benefit of using AWS managed services, such as Amazon ElastiCache and Amazon Relational Database Service (Amazon RDS)?

A. They require the customer to monitor and replace failing instances.

B. They have better performance than customer-managed services.

C. They simplify patching and updating underlying OSs.

D. They do not require the customer to optimize instance type or size selections.

Answer: C. They simplify patching and updating underlying OSs.

193. Which service provides a virtually unlimited amount of online highly durable object storage?

A. Amazon Redshift

B. Amazon Elastic File System (Amazon EFS)

C. Amazon Elastic Container Service (Amazon ECS)

D. Amazon S3

Answer: D. Amazon S3

194. Which of the following Identity and Access Management (IAM) entities is associated with an access key ID and secret access key when using AWS Command Line Interface (AWS CLI)?

    A. IAM group

    B. IAM user

    C. IAM role

    D. IAM policy

Answer: B. IAM user

195. Which of the following security-related services does AWS offer? (Choose two.)

    A. Multi-factor authentication physical tokens

    B. AWS Trusted Advisor security checks

    C. Data encryption

    D. Automated penetration testing

    E. Amazon S3 copyrighted content detection

Answer: B C

196. Which AWS managed service is used to host databases?

    A. AWS Batch

    B. AWS Artifact

    C. AWS Data Pipeline

    D. Amazon RDS

Answer: D. Amazon RDS

197. Which AWS service provides a simple and scalable shared file storage solution for use with Linux-based AWS and on-premises servers?

    A. Amazon S3

    B. Amazon Glacier

    C. Amazon Elastic Block Store (Amazon EBS)

    D. Amazon Elastic File System (Amazon EFS)

Answer: D. Amazon Elastic File System (Amazon EFS)

198. When architecting cloud applications, which of the following are a key design principle?

    A. Use the largest instance possible

    B. Provision capacity for peak load

    C. Use the Scrum development process

    D. Implement elasticity

Answer: D. Implement elasticity

199. Which AWS service should be used for long-term, low-cost storage of data backups?

    A. Amazon RDS

    B. Amazon Glacier

    C. AWS Snowball

    D. AWS EBS

Answer: B. Amazon Glacier

200. Under the shared responsibility model, which of the following is a shared control between a customer and AWS?

    A. Physical controls

    B. Patch management

    C. Zone security

    D. Data center auditing

Answer: B. Patch management

Printed in Great Britain
by Amazon

27356342R00046